TOPIC BOX

The Seasons

Claire Llewellyn

Wayland

Titles in this series
Castles
Dinosaurs
Fairs and Circuses
Houses and Homes
Minibeasts
My Body
The Seasons
Transport

This book was prepared for Wayland (Publishers) Ltd
by Globe Education, Nantwich, Cheshire

Design concept by Pinpoint
Book design by Stephen Wheele Design
Artwork by Colin Newman

First published in 1995 by
Wayland (Publishers) Ltd
61 Western Road, Hove
East Sussex BN3 1JD

© Copyright 1995 Wayland (Publishers) Ltd

Printed and bound in Italy by
L. E. G. O. S.p.A., Vincenza

British Library Cataloguing in Publication Data

Llewellyn, Claire
The Seasons. – (Topic Box Series)
I. Title II. Series
592

ISBN 0 7502 1605 0

Picture acknowledgements

Angus Blackburn cover
Bruce Coleman 7 (Thomas Buchholz), 14 (John Shaw), 26 (Martini), 29 (Dieter and Mary Plage)
Ecoscene 11 (Cooper), 16 (David Purslow), 18 Nick Hawkes, 23 (Cooper)
Life File 24 (S Kay)
Martyn Chillmaid 8
Oxford Scientific films 1 and 10 (J A L Cooke)
NHPA 9 (G J Cambridge), 15 (John Shaw), 19 (Rich Kichner), 22 (T Kitchin and V Hurst), 25 (B and C Alexander)
Robert Harding 12t, 12b
Tony Stone 4 (Jo Browne/Mick Smee), 16/17 (John Chard), 20 (Frank Cezus), 20/21 (Alain Le Garameur), Tony Stone (Ben Osborne)

Contents

The Four Seasons

In many places around the world there are four seasons in the year – spring, summer, autumn and winter.

Each season brings changes in the weather and the time that it gets light in the morning and dark at night. These are big changes, but they take place so slowly that we only notice them a little at a time. Animals and plants feel them too, and their lives change as the seasons move from one to another.

(Right) As the year moves on, the weather changes. Warmer months are followed by colder months. Many plants change the way they grow in each season.

For a few months of the year, the days are long, light and warm. It's summer.

Spring: the first
flowers appear.

Summer: the trees are
in full leaf.

Autumn: many trees start
to lose their leaves.

Winter: nothing grows
and many trees are bare.

Calendar of the Seasons

What Causes Seasons?

The seasons change because of the way the Earth moves around the sun. The Earth's pathway round the sun is called its orbit, and each orbit takes a year from start to finish.

The Earth is tilted in its orbit. At different times, first one pole and then the other leans towards the sun.

When the north pole leans towards the sun, the northern half of the Earth has summer. Meanwhile, the southern half of the Earth is leaning away and has winter.

In June, the northern half of the Earth is leaning towards the sun and has summer.

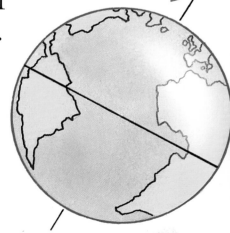

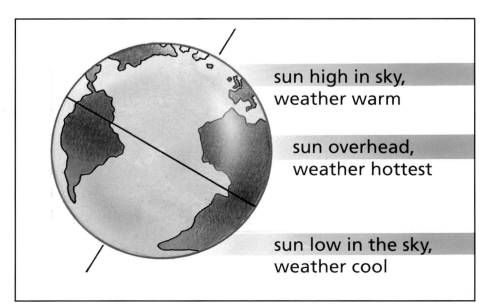

sun high in sky, weather warm

sun overhead, weather hottest

sun low in the sky, weather cool

The south has winter.

(Left) It is hottest where the sun is overhead.

(Left) Shadows are long in winter because even at midday the sun is low in the sky.

(Below) The seasons change as the Earth orbits the sun.

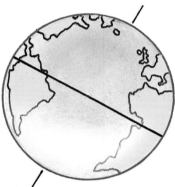

In March, there is spring in the north . . .

. . . and autumn in the south.

In December, the northern half of the Earth is leaning away from the sun and has winter.

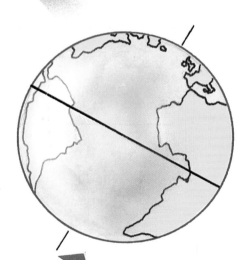

sun

The southern half has summer.

In October, there is autumn in the north and spring in the south.

In March and October, neither half leans towards to sun.

It's Spring!

In spring it gets light a little earlier each morning. Every day, the sun climbs higher in the sky. The weather is brighter and not so cold.

In gardens and fields, the soil warms up slowly. Tiny seedlings start to shoot, buds open, and leaves and flowers begin to grow.

(Right) Spring is a time for planting. Flower and vegetable seeds begin to sprout in the warmer soil. They'll soon start to grow.

(Left) Bulbs sprout under the soil before winter arrives. In spring they grow leaves and buds. Their flowers open in the warm sunshine.

The smallest garden comes to life in the spring. After the cold days of winter, it's good to get outside again.

Animals in Springtime

Like an alarm clock, spring wakes up the animals that slept through the cold days of winter. Insects, spiders, snails and worms are all on the move again. Larger animals snap them up hungrily.

Many animals breed in the spring. There are lambs in the fields, tadpoles in the canal, and ducklings on the river. Winter days are a long way off, and there will be plenty for the young ones to eat in the coming months.

(Right) Young mammals feed on their mother's milk. This helps them to grow quickly.

(Left) Birds build nests in spring, and lay their eggs. They only take a few weeks to hatch.

In springtime,
hungry animals crawl out
from their winter shelter.
They graze on the new grass,
or feed on grubs and insects.
Birds gather twigs
for their nests.

Summer Days

Slowly, as the weeks pass, the days grow longer and the weather gets warmer. In some places, the sun shines every day from sunrise to sunset. Summer evenings are long and late, and the nights are short.

It's harder to work when it's warm, and most of us prefer to be out of doors. Summer is a time for picnics in the park or holidays by the sea. Wherever you go, take care to protect your skin – it burns easily in the sun.

It's fun to eat out of doors. Cafés have tables on the pavement, with large umbrellas to protect you from the sun's glare.

(Left) It's cooler by the sea. The water is refreshing, and there's usually a breeze.

In the flower beds, bees and butterflies fly from one flower to another, feeding on the sugar-sweet nectar.

Summer in the city can be hot and uncomfortable. Away from the traffic, there are cool parks with soft grass and shady trees.

Warmth and Light

The bright warm days make plants grow quickly. The trees are full and green. Their leaves stretch up towards the sun, and use its light to make food for the tree.

On farms, fruit and vegetables begin to ripen. In the fields, the new grass is long and lush. The farmer cuts it, leaves it to dry in the sun, and stores it safely in a barn. The animals will be glad of it in the winter.

plums

raspberries

gooseberries

Young animals are big enough now to leave their nest. They start to learn about the world around them.

14

(Left) Bees can't help getting pollen on themselves when they crawl over a flower. Carrying pollen from flower to flower helps the plants to make seeds.

apricots

cherries

blackcurrants

summer flowers

strawberries

Warm summer days are a time of plenty. Soft fruits are sweet and juicy, and flowers are in full bloom.

Autumn is Here

Slowly, the days grow shorter and cooler. The mornings and evenings are chilly now, and the sun is lower in the sky.

Farmers are harvesting their crops, and storing them carefully in the dry. On bushes and trees there are ripe berries ready for picking.

The leaves are turning brown. They feel dry, and start to fall from the branch. Many trees lose their leaves in winter. It helps them to survive the cold.

Trees that lose their leaves are called deciduous. Before the leaves fall, they change their colour from green to red, yellow or brown.

(Left) The weather is changing. Late autumn brings grey skies and rain. This is often a time of storms.

Berries and nuts ripen. They are food for many animals, and their seeds may grow into new plants next year.

Mushrooms and other fungi grow in damp corners among the leaves.

In autumn, plants and animals begin to prepare for winter.

Looking Ahead

The shorter duller days give an important signal – summer is over, and winter is on the way.

Wild animals fatten up before the cold weather arrives. There is plenty of food to eat, and some animals bury a little extra for the cold days ahead. Their warm coats begin to thicken, and some of them even start to change colour. A white coat is useful in the winter – it helps to hide an animal once the snow starts to fall.

The trees are bare.

It's not hard to find food in autumn. Ripe nuts fall to the ground in their thousands.

(Below) It's getting cold, and people are spending more time indoors. Outside, the world gets ready for winter.

(Above) The snowshoe hare lives in Canada. Its white winter coat starts growing in the autumn. This will hide the animal from owls and foxes in the snow.

Most animals are well fed.

Old leaves and stems are thrown on the bonfire.

Many plants die back after the first frosts.

It's Winter Now

Winter days are dark and short. The sun feels weak, and casts long shadows. Winter nights are cold and frosty, and there is ice in the morning.

Very cold weather makes it hard to get about. Snowdrifts block the roads, and in the coldest places, frozen rivers keep ships stranded in the ports.

Most people prefer to stay inside now. They wear extra clothes, turn up the heating, and eat plenty of hot food to keep themselves warm.

Just a little snow can bring traffic to a standstill. In some places, where winters are hard, drivers put chains on their tyres so that the wheels grip the road.

(Left) In North America, many ships sail to ports along the St Lawrence River. But the water freezes over in winter, and the ships can't get in or out.

Hungry owls hunt during daylight.

People build homes that keep them in the warm.

Snowmobiles run on skis rather than wheels and are a good way to get around in the snow.

(Above) Winters are even colder in the mountains.

Surviving the Winter

Winter is the hardest season for living things. Nothing grows in the frozen soil, but roots and seeds manage to survive underground. Only a few trees are still green. They have tough waxy needles or leaves that can stand the winter cold.

kestrel

Food and water are so hard to find that some animals hibernate through the coldest months. Others brave the winter chill, but it's a hard time and many of them grow thin and hungry.

Wolves live were winters are cold. They shelter in the forests, and grow thick coats to keep out the cold.

blackbird

badgers

(Right) Tiny bodies are hard to keep warm. Birds fluff up their feathers to trap air inside. This warms them like a feather quilt.

squirrel

fox

mouse

toad

hedgehog

rabbits

Woods are quiet in winter. Many of the animals are hibernating but others are just resting. Hibernating animals find a warm safe place and sleep until the spring. There are few signs of life – nothing for a hungry fox to eat.

23

Following the Seasons

Year in, year out, the seasons follow each other in a never-ending pattern. Thousands of years ago, people's lives began to follow this pattern. Farmers studied the sun and stars to find out when to sow and harvest their crops.

Even today, some people still live by the seasons. Every spring, Lapp herders follow their reindeer as they leave the forests and migrate further north. And in the autumn, when the animals return, they follow them back.

Nomads in Iran follow their animals as they search for fresh grazing. In summer, they climb higher in the mountains. In winter, they come down to the valleys.

(Right) Lapps depend on reindeer for food and skins. When the reindeer migrate to new feeding grounds in the spring and autumn, the Lapp herders follow them.

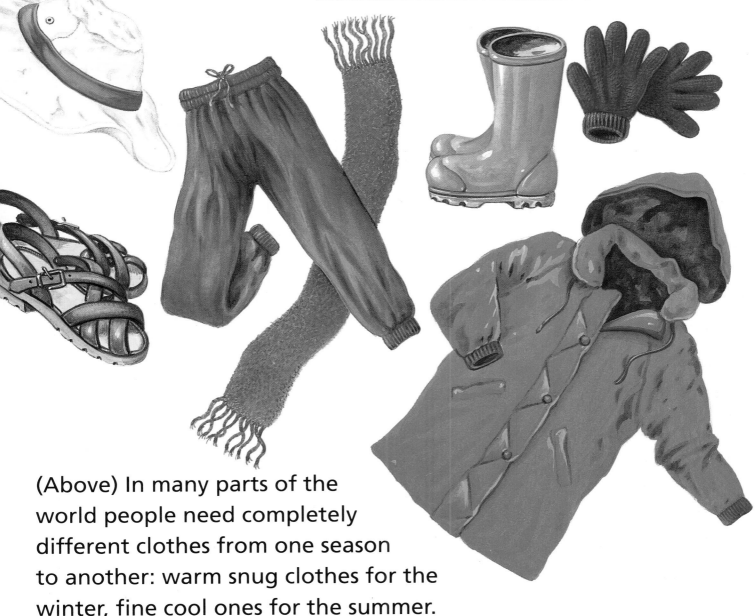

(Above) In many parts of the world people need completely different clothes from one season to another: warm snug clothes for the winter, fine cool ones for the summer.

Farming Seasons

The farming year follows the pattern of the seasons. It starts in early spring when farmers plough their fields and prepare them for planting. In summer the farmers work long hours making hay, and spraying and harvesting their crops.

For other farmers the year starts with the birth of lambs and calves. The growing animals graze on the hills during the summer, but farmers bring them back down to the farm when the weather grows cold.

(Left) By early autumn, bunches of grapes have ripened in the vineyards. They are picked, ready for making wine.

In summer, the growing crops are sprayed to protect them from harmful insects and disease. The animals graze on the lush grass.

In spring, the farmers prepare the fields and sow their crops. It's still cold when the calves and lambs are born.

The farming year.

In autumn, the crops are harvested and stored under cover. The animals are brought down closer to the farm.

In winter, the bare fields are ploughed ready for the spring. The grass stops growing and the animals feed on dry hay.

Other Seasons

Not everywhere in the world has four seasons. Near the equator, the weather is never cold, and the days and nights hardly change. But for half the year winds blow in from the sea bringing rain. This gives many countries just two seasons – one wet and one dry.

At the poles the weather is cold all the year, but there is a change in the days and nights. In summer, the sun never sets. In winter, it never rises. There are two seasons – one light, one dark.

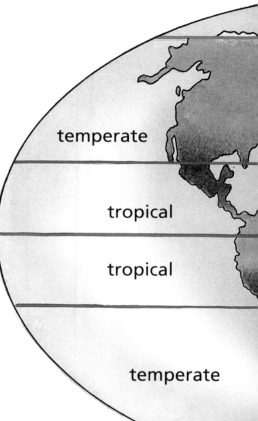

temperate

tropical

tropical

temperate

(Left) The weather in Antarctica is always cold but it warms up a little in the summer months when the sun never sets.

(Right) Heavy monsoon rains are carried on winds from the sea. They blow across countries near to the equator during the summer months.

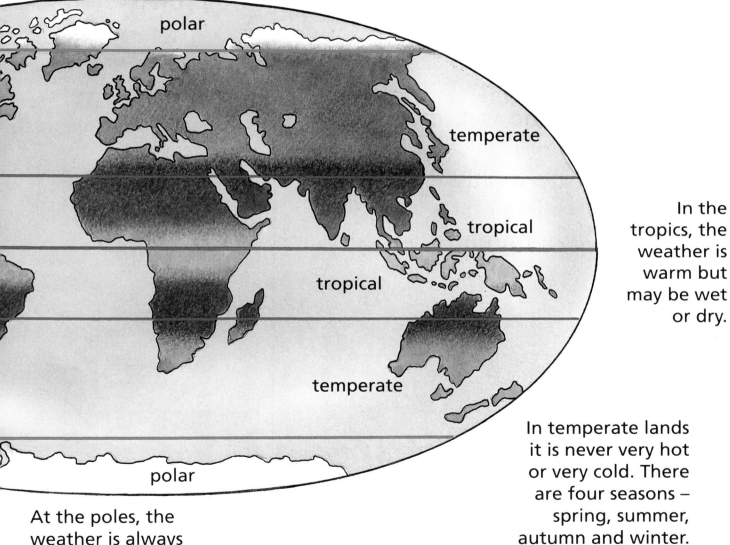

polar

temperate

tropical

In the tropics, the weather is warm but may be wet or dry.

tropical

temperate

polar

In temperate lands it is never very hot or very cold. There are four seasons – spring, summer, autumn and winter.

At the poles, the weather is always cold but the days are light in summer and dark in winter.

(Above) As you travel from the tropics to the poles the weather changes – and so do the seasons.

29

Word List

Antarctica   A huge piece of land at the south pole. It is the coldest place on Earth.

Bulb   Plants such as daffodils and onions grow from bulbs underground. It is the plump part of a plant where food is stored in the winter.

Conifer   A tree that has cones and tough needles instead of leaves. Most conifers keep their needles all through the winter.

Equator   An imaginary line around the fattest part of the Earth, halfway between the north and south poles.

Fungi   Very simple plants that do not have proper stems, leaves or flowers. Mushrooms and moulds are kinds of fungi.

Grub   The tiny creatures that hatch out from the eggs of beetles and flies.

Hibernate   To sleep during the winter.

Lapp   A person who lives in Lapland – the coldest, most northern parts of Finland, Sweden and Norway. Some Lapps are nomads.

Mammal   Warm-blooded animals that feed their young on milk. Humans are also mammals.

Migrate   To travel from one place to another at certain times of year to breed or find food.

Monsoon   A tropical wind that blows from the sea to the land during summer. It brings heavy rains to countries near the Equator.

Nectar   A sweet juice that is made by flowers and collected by bees and other insects.

Nomad   A person who travels from place to place to find grass for their animals.

Orbit   An orbit is the path of one object travelling around another. The moon orbits the Earth; the Earth orbits the sun.

Plough   To dig over the soil and break it up, ready for planting.

Poles   The most northern and southern parts of the Earth.

Pollen   A yellow dust that is made by flowers, and which helps to make seeds.

Ray   The sun's light travels in straight lines called rays.

Seedling   The thin young plant that grows from a seed.

Snowmobile   A vehicle with an engine that travels on snow. It has skis instead of wheels.

Temperate   Temperate lands lie between the tropics and the poles.

Tropical   Tropical lands lie near the Equator.

Valley   The low ground that lies between two hills or mountains.

Vineyard   A farm where grapes are planted.

Finding Out More

Places to Visit

Any or all of the following at different times of the year:

farms and farmland,

moorland and heathland,

nature trails and reserves,

parks and gardens,

sites of special scientific interest,

woodlands and forests.

Books to Read

Changing Seasons, Henry Pluckrose, (Watts, 1993)

Clothes Around the World, Godfrey Hall, (Wayland, 1995)

Eyewitness Explorers: Weather, and *Eyewitness Explorers: Flowers*, (Dorling Kindersley, 1992)

Food Around the World, Godfrey Hall, (Wayland, 1995)

Get set... Go: The Seasons series, four titles, Ruth Thomson, (Watts)

Looking at Weather, Gary Gibson (Watts, 1995)

Pond Year, Kathryn Lasky and Mike Bostock, (Walker Books, 1995)

The Seasons, Joy Richardson, (Watts, 1991)

Weather Watch series, four titles, Miriam Moss (Wayland, 1994)

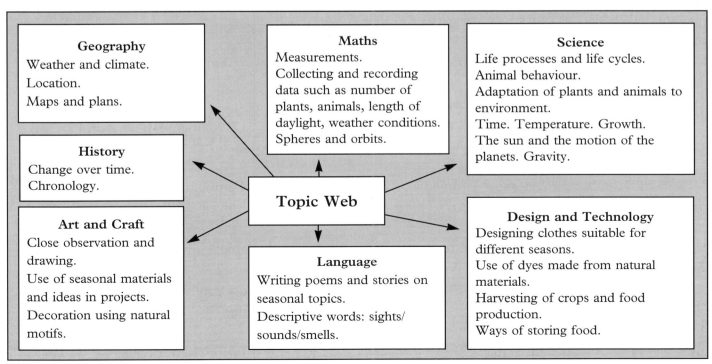

Geography
Weather and climate.
Location.
Maps and plans.

Maths
Measurements.
Collecting and recording data such as number of plants, animals, length of daylight, weather conditions.
Spheres and orbits.

Science
Life processes and life cycles.
Animal behaviour.
Adaptation of plants and animals to environment.
Time. Temperature. Growth.
The sun and the motion of the planets. Gravity.

History
Change over time.
Chronology.

Topic Web

Design and Technology
Designing clothes suitable for different seasons.
Use of dyes made from natural materials.
Harvesting of crops and food production.
Ways of storing food.

Art and Craft
Close observation and drawing.
Use of seasonal materials and ideas in projects.
Decoration using natural motifs.

Language
Writing poems and stories on seasonal topics.
Descriptive words: sights/sounds/smells.

Index